The Haitian-Creole Alphabets
Alfabè Kreyòl Ayisyen Yo

by Berwick Augustin

© Copyright 2021 by Berwick Augustin
Published by Evoke180 Publishing
www.evoke180.com

All rights reserved. Except as permitted under the U.S. Copyright Act of 1976, no part of this publication may be reproduced, distributed, stored in a retrieval system, or transmitted in any form or by any means- electronic, mechanical, digital, photocopy, recording, or any other except for brief quotations in printed reviews, without the prior written permission of the publisher.

Printed in the United States of America
Designed and illustrated by Merline Labissiere

Translated by Evoke180
ISBN-13- 978-1733076760

A people without language is a nation without culture and identity.

Yon pèp san lang se yon nasyon san kilti ak idantite.

~Berwick Augustin

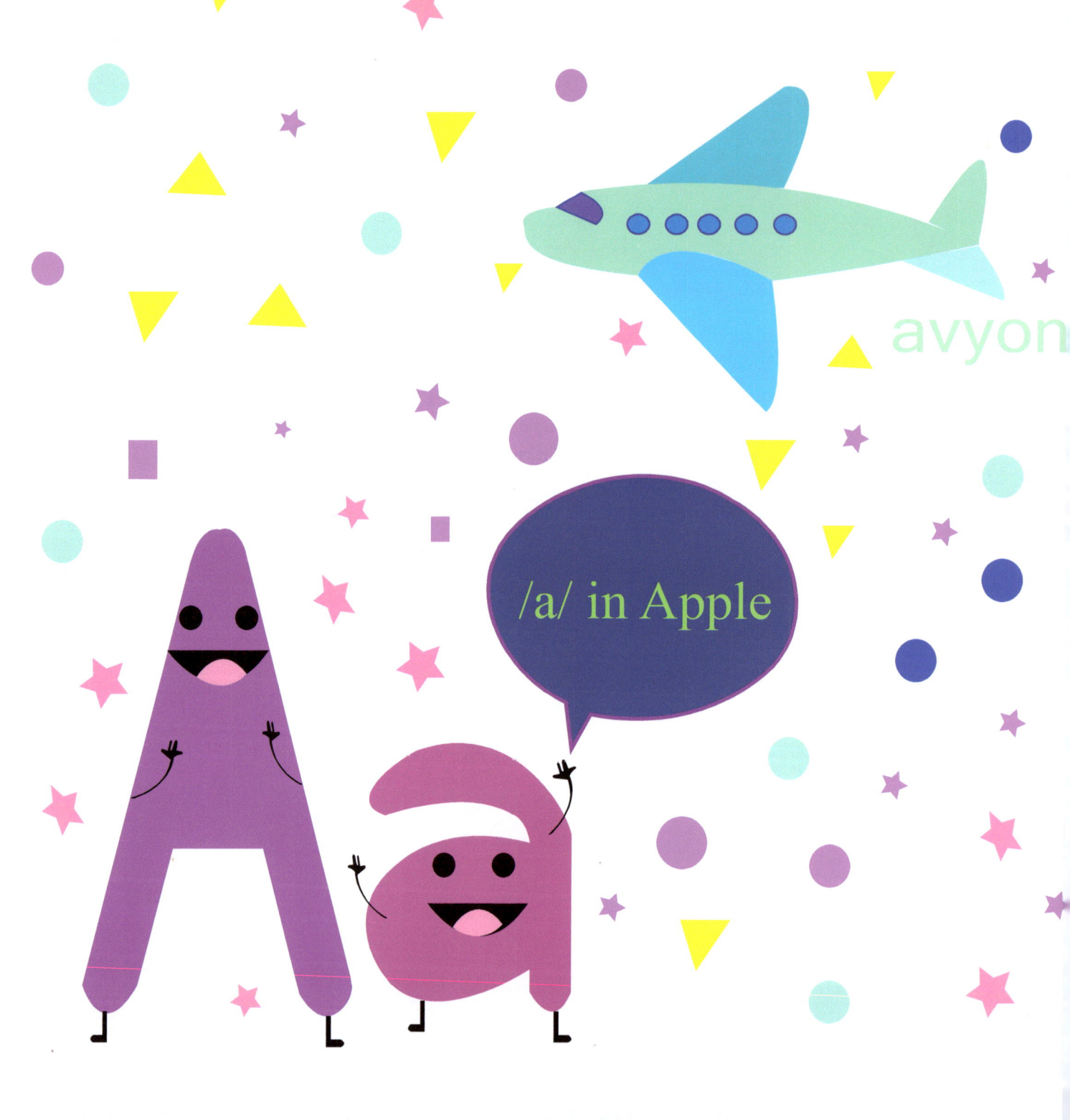

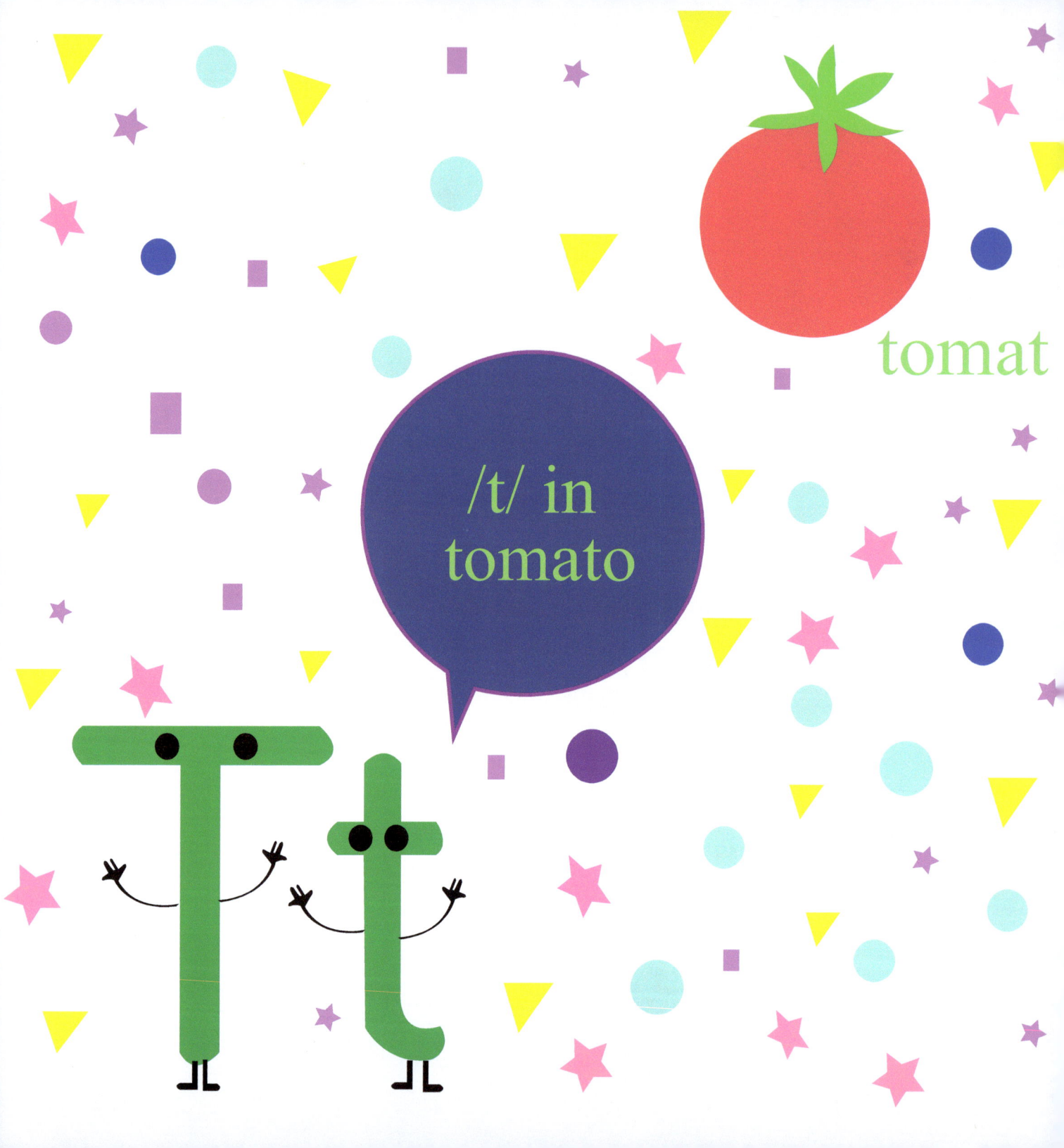

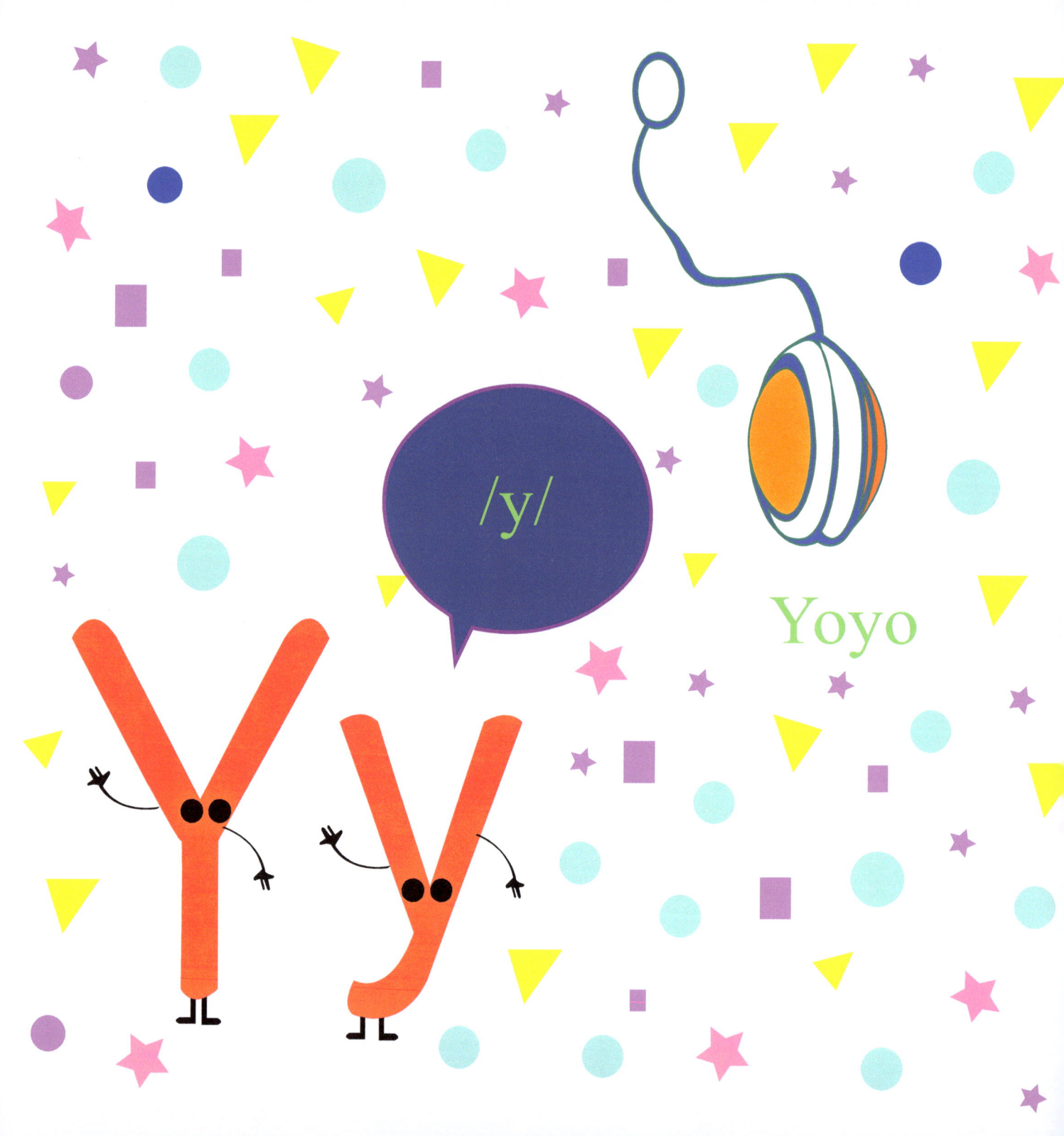

Also by Berwick Augustin

symbolism of the Haitian flag.
Children's Historical Fiction/ 978-0-9991822-1-5

Battaille de Vertiteres to fulfill his soccer dreams.
Children's Historical Fiction/ 978-1795490771

1803 SERIES WORKBOOKS (Student & Teacher's Editions)

The 1803 workbooks are designed to help young learners from K-12 practice the skills that are demanded of today's standards. Students will draw, write, create, and apply developmentally appropriate reading skills while using text-based evidence to answer questions.

Also by Berwick Augustin

The Lord's Prayer- Lapriye Senyè a

The Lord's Prayer is one of many ancient examples from Jesus on how to pray intimately and effectively to the father. This powerful passage is all inclusive with themes of worship, forgiveness, repentance, and provision. This children's book embodies Jesus' call to "let the little children come to Him." Berwick Augustin weaves his faith and culture into this bilingual book to creatively help parents teach their children the Lord's prayer and the many lessons within it. In this book, you will find delightful illustrations, English and Haitian Creole text, and discussion questions to empower all children to know that God created them just as they are.

Children's Spiritual/978-1-7330767-1-5

Numbered Words

Words are powerful! They can either breathe or suffocate life. Many times wordiness can defeat the effectiveness of a message. This book is designed to convey succinct poems packed with powerful lessons. The poem's numerical number determines the amount of words it contains; the first one has 1 word while the fiftieth poem has 50 words.

Poetry/978-0999182208

 Evoke180 Publishing